The Craighead Christmas Messages

Paul D. McDonagh

2019ISBN: 9781693556098

For those who want to keep Christmas throughout the year

For the people of Craighead Housing Estate, Barrhead

G.K. Chesterton

"Christmas is built upon a beautiful and intentional paradox; that the birth of the homeless should be celebrated in every home."

CONTENTS

Lewis Carroll

"I wonder if the snow loves the trees and fields, that it kisses them so gently? And then it covers them up snug, you know, with a white quilt; and perhaps it says, 'go to sleep, darlings, till the summer comes again.'"

Introduction

I began writing the first Craighead Christmas message on the back of several community projects I organised across Barrhead. Over the years, many people have told me how much they enjoyed reading the Craighead Christmas messages. Indeed, a young man about nineteen years of age came up to me and said that the Christmas message I wrote that year saved his life. My message stopped him from committing suicide. Of course, the truth is he saved himself. I merely gave him something that inspired him to find the strength to keep going and confront his troubles.

I never imagined anything I wrote would help save a life, but I recognise that Christmas is quite a lonely and isolating time of the year for many people. It is why I began this project and continue to write a Craighead Christmas message every year. I also write the occasional Craighead Hogmanay message, so you'll find copies of them included here.

It only costs me around £50-£100 to buy 500 Christmas cards and print out 500 copies of the Christmas message every year. I have made a real difference for such a small amount of money. I hope these messages from Christmas past inspire you to write your own Christmas message this year and print copies for your friends, family and neighbours to read. You may even save a life. Of course, there's no reason for you to print out as many copies as I do. After all, you may live in a small street with just a few houses. But it is vital that you pick up your pen if you feel you could help others in this way.

In the end, I hope the Craighead Christmas messages and inspirational quotes in this book help you in some small way. I hope they make your Christmas a happy one.

Merry Christmas

Paul D. McDonagh
on behalf of the tenants and residents of Craighead Housing Estate.

THE NEIGHBOURS
Paul D. McDonagh

It wasn't in what they said
but in what they did
that proved to her
she belonged.

The comforting word
when grief was at its worst,
the offer of help freely given,
the simple decency that wasn't showy
like the rich man at the poor box,
but more like the poor widow
who had nothing but gave her all.

Charles Baudelaire

"We are weighed down, every moment, by the conception and the sensation of Time. And there are but two means of escaping and forgetting this nightmare: pleasure and work. Pleasure consumes us. Work strengthens us. Let us choose."

1

Craighead Christmas Message 2012

Who you are and what you do matters! Unlike the character Scrooge, most of us will never get the opportunity to save the life of a sick child. Most of us will never, thankfully, have to choose to stand in front of a man with a gun to protect young children as a teacher did recently. But every single one of us will at some point come to realise a fundamental truth of human existence: we make a difference in the lives of our friends, family and neighbours every day with a kind word or a helpful action.

The neighbour who helps a mother carry her pram up a flight of stairs or the person who takes out the bins for their elderly neighbours, through their actions, make the lives of those around them more bearable. It's an essential truth of life that our choices and decisions determine our character and affect those around us.

In the hurly-burly of daily life, we don't have time to reflect on who we are and what we want. But just like Scrooge, we're haunted at this time of year by the Ghosts of Christmas. They remind us that no matter our choices, we can still choose to act differently in the present, and by changing ourselves, we have an impact on our friends, family and community. In the year ahead, may the chains of friendship weigh lightly upon you and bind you close to your friends, your family, and to those you have chosen to share your life with.

BARRHEAD AND NEILSTON DISABLED FORUM
Paul D. McDonagh

Charlie pushes a wheelchair
and places an old woman
next to a man with cards.
A lady with legs made useless
by time smiles as she sips her tea
and remembers working in a convent.

An old man bites into a biscuit
his dentures rub at his gums;
he growls from behind newsprint.
His hands once hard as spades
have been made weak with age;
the newspaper shakes in the air.

Charlie weaves a tea trolley through
the maze of tables and old chairs.
The noise of ageing voices laughing
fills the room with quiet history for no one
will record what is written in old men;
Charlie sits down, still smiling for them.

Someone comes and asks him, 'Are you okay?'
'Aye, I'm fine, love. I was resting.'
And then he's up quickly again pushing
wheelchairs about with a smile on his face,
a glint in his eyes and his heart medicine
safely in his pocket resting, just resting.

The Ghost of Jacob Marley

"Business! Mankind was my business. The common welfare was my business; charity, mercy, forbearance, and benevolence, were, all, my business. The dealings of my trade were but a drop of water in the comprehensive ocean of my business!"

2

Craighead Christmas Message 2013

A couple of weeks ago we turned on our TV screens and saw the after-effects of a helicopter crash in Glasgow. We may have tried to make sense of this event in our quiet moments. Our thoughts may have turned to the plight of those families affected by tragedy so close to Christmas. Unlike many of us, they must face the pain and anguish of such a sudden and unexpected loss. They must face the silence created by the vacant space at their Christmas dinner. And they will suffer from the pain inflicted upon them by their love; they will hold the presents bought for their loved ones and know that those they have lost will never come back. Only memories will remain amongst the gifts left unopened near a Christmas tree.

In imagining the grief of these families, we can become overwhelmed by the brutal, unpredictable and absurd qualities of life and death. But even in the shadow of tragedy, we can still find that quiet light hidden in the ordinary decent person. Those in the pub did not run for their lives; instead, they stayed to rescue friends and strangers alike; doctors and nurses, not on duty, turned up to offer their help to the injured, and hundreds of ordinary Glaswegians that are just like you took the time to donate their blood.

As horrible as this tragedy has been, there is a fundamental truth evident in the actions of our fellow citizens: something beautiful and life-affirming is alive in the human heart. And although human life is both fragile and finite, and although the manner of our death may be unpredictable, we know that we are linked together by the chains of our common humanity: we are bound to each other and share a common journey. This truth compels us to connect with those around us, especially at Christmas. This truth reminds us that, although we have made mistakes in our past and may make more in the years ahead, we all have the opportunity, in the time left to us, to overcome our failings and make a difference in the lives of others.

We may sometimes forget how powerful we are because our

past, full of disappointment, clouds our thoughts, but we also know the shadows of the future can give way to a life filled with love and meaning. So, although Christmas will never put a scrap of gold in your pocket, I hope, in the year ahead, you can find the spirit of Christmas in those precious moments you spend with others. I hope you are haunted gently by your acts of kindness. In your darkest moments, I hope you remember there is always a way to connect with those around you. I hope you understand that you matter more to those around you than you sometimes realise and that your greatest treasure is not found in how much money you have in the bank but in the love you have to give.

DISAPPOINTMENT
Paul D. McDonagh

I read a poem in which disappointment is incidentally
described as having a knapsack and ragged tent.

It struck me just now, might it also be possible
that it has an unkempt beard and yellow teeth

and a musty pong, which comes from standing around
in the rain while wearing the same clothes

for days. But perhaps disappointment doesn't wear
a human face or have teeth of any sort. Perhaps like hope,

its opposite, it has feathers it uses to fly around
and whack us across the head with its wings of despair.

But perhaps disappointment is none of these things
and simply your hopes for today deferred until tomorrow.

Scan the QR Code to reveal your secret message.

Pope Paul VI

"All life demands struggle. Those who have everything given to them become lazy, selfish, and insensitive to the real values of life. The very striving and hard work that we so constantly try to avoid is the major building block in the person we are today."

3

Craighead Hogmanay Message 2013

As we celebrate the New Year's gift, Hogmanay, we once more engage in a Scottish tradition: we have a big party and drink so much we can't remember a thing. For many of us, the annual editions of *Only an Excuse?* And *Hogmanay Live* will fill the TV screen, providing background noise to the conversations that fill our homes. Some of us may have found 2013 to be as bad as the recent weather. But the dark clouds, which threatened to wash away our happiness in 2013, will recede in the New Year, for no storm, however destructive, lasts forever. As the clouds dissipate and the sun rises in the sky, I hope you find the resolve to meet the goals and resolutions you set for yourself in 2014. Remember, you can make different choices. Life isn't like it is on TV. There is no perfect moment to change your life, but you can still achieve your dreams and overcome all your challenges, but you must do it today. So, do it now.

Ralph Waldo Emmerson

"To laugh often and much; to win the respect of intelligent people and the affection of children; to earn the appreciation of honest critics and endure the betrayal of false friends; to appreciate the beauty; to find the best in others; to leave the world a bit better, whether by a healthy child, a garden patch Or a redeemed social condition; to know even one life has breathed easier because you have lived. This is to have succeeded!"

4

Craighead Christmas Message 2014

For some people, this Christmas will be far from a happy one. Some will experience the breakdown of a long-term relationship or the loss of a close friend or family member. Others filled with worry over a sick child or the prospect of unemployment will find worry robs them of sleep. But instinctively, we know that whatever troubles come our way, we can endure them just as we endured past difficulties.

With its repeats of *It's a Wonderful Life* and *A Christmas Carol*, Christmas may seem overly sentimental, especially when faced with real hardship. But the journey of Scrooge and that of George Bailey remind us of an essential truth. Whatever difficulties we face, whatever calamities life puts in our way, we have a power greater than any president or prime minister.

We may never make it into the history books and never find our simple acts of kindness and bravery being studied by children in school. But we know that, as Scrooge and George Bailey discovered, what we do and who we are matters. We can make a difference in the lives of those around us. The choice we face is not whether to believe this fact but what we decide to do with our power to lighten the burden of those around us.

If your Christmas is one filled with the shadows of the future and the pain of the past, I trust you find the hope within you and let it guide you towards lasting happiness.

A STORY OF HOPE
Paul D. McDonagh

'Hope is the thing with feathers,'
said Emily Dickinson
over one hundred and fifty years ago.

And over two thousand years
earlier a woman with a box,
after unleashing all the evils

into the world, stood beside the Gods
watching as four of the darkest horses
with their skeleton riders rode off,

across the open fields which surrounded
them, leaving a dark trail in their wake.
And once the sound of the laughing

skeletons and thunder of dark hooves
had been dulled into the distance,
a pale half-dead man in a black cloak

with a farmer's scythe pulled himself
out the box, looked at the gods
that stood around him, bowed briefly,

winked as he nodded, and then skipped along
the path before him, whistling a merry tune.
The gods, in their surprise, leaned forward.

They looked deep into Pandora's box,
but having seen everything before,
thought it must be empty. It wasn't.

Inside was the thing with feathers:
a strange creature of flight that has more
in common with the Chimera than with Pegasus.

Hope flew out the box.

It stared into Pandora's eyes for a moment
then flew above their heads and away
towards the sky. Since that day, Hope has flown

into many battlefields - whispered into the ears
of fathers soon to lose their battle with death,
and in the hearts of mothers dying in childbirth.

It whispered the lies: your death has meaning,
your love will survive beyond this moment.
Through the centuries it has visited many

deathbeds, prisons and places of despair,
but still it was never enough. Its feathers,
once mostly white with black around the edges,

became progressively grey. It flew lower
until it found itself unable to remember
flight; the hearts of men beat to despair.

Then it discovered those hands that fought
with pens, not swords and saw, perched
in their words, a way of visiting men

and women on the battlefield of the mind.
Soon it rediscovered how to fly
in the hearts of women living restricted lives,

in men that knew they'd face death too young,
and in the works of all those that imagined
children growing up without love but hoped

for more. Now, it has flown through my window
and nips the soft flesh between my knuckles.
I have been reminded to tell you

since the day that it decided to look

into Pandora's eyes, and saw tears fall
down her cheeks and the gods laughing,

it knew two things: the gods would play with the hearts
of men and women, and it had found its purpose:
it was not here to offer us the truth but knowledge

that whatever games the gods may play
with you, you can endure your suffering
because, unlike them, Hope beats within you.

5

Craighead Hogmanay Message 2014

At the New Year millions of people all over the world sing an old Scottish song, *Auld Lang Syne*. While this song may not be the best in Burns's repertoire, it's a song that strikes a chord with many people from different cultures across the globe. Perhaps this time of the year can inspire us just like the song inspires some people, for hope is at its highest right now. As people begin journeys to change their lives and the lives of those around them, a little piece of Scotland sails with them into the winds of change.

We also know that life will not stand still for us. The question we face, especially at this time of the year, is what kind of change do we want to see? Change will come what may, but we have a choice in the face of the inevitable. Will we become the pebble in a pond causing ripples to the furthest bank? Will we become the butterfly flapping its wings that causes a hurricane halfway around the world, or will we cower like the mouse in one of Burns's better poems, too scared to change yet having change thrust upon us by a murdering pattle?

Of course, you may believe that any change you try to make to your life will be insignificant, but perhaps that's the point. We are all insignificant, but our actions affect the lives of those we love, and collectively our efforts impact the world in a way that we may not fully appreciate. So, whatever New Year resolutions you have, I hope you achieve them, and even if you don't, I hope you find your journey a positive one and that it strengthens your resolve to be the person you are meant to be.

WHATEVER YOU DO
Paul D. McDonagh

"Whatever you do will be insignificant, but it is very important that you do it."
Gandhi

Perhaps he was being humble and far-seeing: one day
he'll become merely a footnote in the history of India
and join the ranks of all those people who have shaped

the world in which we live, but are remembered now
in some obscure article or web page read by students
too busy doing their essays to protest against injustice.

Does he mean you can be the President of America
or even Prime Minister of the United Kingdom,
but no matter what you do it's all equally insignificant

like that drop of water in an ocean, that pebblein a pond
or that frightful butterfly flapping its wings,
causing a hurricane somewhere in the world?

Maybe it's in recognition that all your actions
from tying your shoelaces to wearing a seatbelt
can carry consequences for you and those around you.

Maybe it's to remind you that all the mundane,
ordinary things you do like loving your friends,
hugging your children and reading to them

at night, may not alter the destiny of the cosmos
but only you can do it; the stars can keep
care of themselves, but only you can love

in the way that you do. Maybe he's trying
to help you to not worry about money,
or power, or fame, to remember that life
is like a grain of sand slipping through
the hourglass of time where everything becomes
insignificant in the face of Death's embrace.

"I have always thought of Christmas time as a good time; a kind, forgiving, charitable, pleasant time; the only time I know of, when men and women open their shut-up hearts freely, and think of people below them as if they really were fellow passengers to the grave, and not another race of creatures bound on other journeys. And therefore, uncle, though it has never put a scrap of gold or silver in my pocket, I believe it has done me good, and will do me good; and I say, God bless it!" *Fred, Scrooge's Nephew, A Christmas Carol*

6

Craighead Christmas Message 2015

With terrorist groups like Islamic State and the recent flooding in Cumbria hitting the headlines, it is easy to give in to the feeling that the human race is going to hell in a handcart. It's easy to give in to the feeling that, even if the terrorists aren't victorious, the damage done to the environment will cause our downfall. And it's easy to look at the world and bear witness to the suffering of others and then give into the belief that perhaps we aren't worth saving, that perhaps the human race is damned. And yet, in our despair, there is a greater truth. It is not the cruelty and brutality of groups like Islamic State that's stronger, but you. It is your empathy, your ability to be moved by the plight of strangers who are forced to flee their homes because of floods or war, which is far more powerful. It is your thoughts and actions which reveal something quite remarkable is alive in the human heart. The world can be a cruel and brutal place. But it's filled with millions of ordinary decent people like you who recognise our shared humanity and are moved by the suffering they see around them. You recognise that hell isn't a place but is, in fact, the feeling you must confront when you see the suffering of others and know there is nothing you can do to stop it, especially if it is someone close to you.

You may not think that your ability to empathise, to feel the suffering of others, is all that remarkable, but it is. What's more, you have gotten up every day this year, despite your pain and suffering, and done your best for your friends and family. In the face of your despair and disappointment, you keep trying, however imperfectly, to live a life filled with love and common decency. So be kind to yourself. I hope you come to realise that just like the character George Bailey in *It's a Wonderful Life,* you have a powerful impact on those around you. And just like George Bailey, I guess you probably haven't stopped to think that you deserve to be loved just as much as you love those around you. There are no angels like Clarence able and willing to show you how the world would be a poorer place without you, though I hope, despite your struggles, you still dare to have dreams and the wisdom to pursue them. This year may have been full of suffering and disappointment, but you have weathered the storms.

You are still standing, still alive. And most of all, you can still make
a difference. You can act with kindness and compassion towards those
you meet because your life is the beacon in the darkness.

SIGNS OF BELONGING
Paul D. McDonagh

The tenements of Craigheads
nest amongst the trees.
Grey roofs and white roughcasting,

these seagulls are too fixed for the sea,
yet they still flap with open windows.
Music shuffles the air with new dreams

to fill walkways with rap and hip-hop
which mingles into the easy listening
of children laughing with full throats.

Considered too young for the park,
they play on the patches of grass
in full view of their anxious mothers.

Beyond the wheelie bins and the comfort
of an old sofa that waits to be skipped,
the park across the road is full of boys

who kick an old football around for fun.
Here the Old Firm have to play together
to make up the numbers. Winning now

relies on passing to names, not to colours
worn like articles of faith by weary men
too used for hope and too dead to dream.

A girl in a sari sits on a swing texting;
a wee nipper twitters as she slides down
a chute giggling. Freewheelers pass through

flying towards the shop full of small things.
An old man exits with newspapers and cigarettes;
his jacket is warm and too heavy for the weather.
The boys, their mountain bikes parked unchained,

have bought their cokes and sit a moment to talk
of school, girls, football and other stuff.

Then they're off, up Springhill Road to the Dams
or the Jerries where old graffiti still holds meaning,
and the sound of their voices echo under a viaduct.

Meanwhile, the shopkeeper on his mobile speaks Urdu
to his gran. He smiles back to the guy that's just bought
a Pot Noodle, and asks him, 'How's your grandad?'

Outside a kid struggles with a Tesco bag full of bottles
empty of Irn Bru, but still worth the effort he thinks;
he drags them in to redeem their value in sweets.

And then it's quiet for a while, except for seagulls
that sing to each other from the roofs - ready for the sea.
A priest, having visited an old man close to death,

walks in to pick up his newspaper and Lucozade,
as he pays, he says hesitantly, 'Peace be upon you,'
and Tariq replies: 'And peace be upon you also, Father.'

Aesop

"No act of kindness, no matter how small, is ever wasted."

7

Craighead Christmas Message 2016

With the election of Donald Trump and the result of the Brexit vote, you'd be forgiven for thinking there's not much to be cheerful about this Christmas. It seems some very dark forces are stalking the world. As hard as it can be to see the silver lining at the moment, there is cause for hope if you look closely enough.

Men like Donald Trump and Nigel Farage have channelled the most cynical and destructive forces of the human spirit and gained popularity. But it's still possible to direct the same discontent to achieve great things that lift people's spirits. It's still possible to bind ourselves towards a common purpose that enriches our lives. You only have to look at Martin Luther King and Gandhi to see what's possible in our crazy, mixed-up world. Both these men overcame overwhelming odds to achieve freedom and dignity for those they represented, and they did this without appealing to destructive emotions like hate and fear.

The truth of this year is self-evident – the elites that govern us have a lot of power, but they can only wield that power with our consent, especially in a democracy. There are, after all, more people like us in the world than rich people. The most profound lesson of history is that the elites often forget their place. They forget that they serve the poor and the marginalised. If they do not understand this, the poor and marginalised will punish them at the ballot box and give those that presume to govern us their marching orders. We have long memories, and sometimes we aren't in a forgiving mood. Donald Trump in America and Nigel Farage in the UK, and what they represent, are a warning shot across the bows of those who have failed to govern justly. They ignore this warning, ignore you at their peril.

The Labour government of 1945 built the NHS, the Welfare State and thousands of council houses at a time when the British economy was a mess from the aftermath of war, and the population was still subject to rationing. If a Labour government could do all that in the grip of real austerity, surely the current government can do better. In a time when the austerity we suffer from is a consequence of mistakes made by bankers and the elites enthralled by them, we can and must do better. There are no more excuses left for those who govern us. If they are unwilling to heed the warnings, then we are doomed.

Of course, the truth is, whether you are a billionaire or a bin man, each of us has the power to change the world. Now, that's something worth reflecting on this Christmas as we chart a course between hope and disappointment.

LIKE SISYPHUS
Paul D. McDonagh

Sisyphus the king was punished by the gods,
was made to roll a boulder up a hill
time and time again only to watch it
roll back down again.

Perhaps you and your mates
shook your heads and sighed
when you had one of those days:
the clouds were threatening rain
and a kid had drawn over
a wall freshly painted or nicked
a tin of paint and decided to do something
unmentionable with one of the rollers.

But then again, maybe you smiled
as I imagine Sisyphus may have done
despite the task before him
because he heard the birds sing to him
from the trees or because he knew
even if the boulder rolled away again
at least he'd still have the view
which would always be worth the effort
even if the boulder wasn't.

And like Sisyphus perhaps you smiled
not because you knew there was nothing
you could do, so it was better to laugh than cry.
No, you smiled like Sisyphus
because you discovered something

others never come to know.

It does not matter if your task
must be repeated time and time again
because even if you must do the same thing
every day it will always be different
for you will change and the world
will change with you, too.

The Ghost of Jacob Marley

"It is required of every man that the spirit within him should walk abroad among his fellow men and travel far and wide; and if that spirit goes not forth in life, it is condemned to do so after death... and witness what it cannot share, but might have shared and turned to happiness."

8

Craighead Christmas Message 2017

In a year in which public figures have been embroiled in yet another scandal involving the abuse of power, it is hard to see the beacon in the darkness. It is hard to see the light still shining beyond the litany of sexual harassment allegations that seem symptomatic of a broader malaise in our culture. That victims have finally been listened to should give us cause for hope. It would be worse if power were wielded to cover up these incidents as in the past.

Those who have endured the injustices perpetrated by influential people may have suffered for many years, but they found the courage to speak out against those who would silence them. They found out that they were not as alone as they thought. And nor are you.

You may have a petty tyrant for a boss or be in an unequal or abusive relationship, but you are not alone, and you can take the next step towards freedom if only you dare to dream of the life you deserve.

The truth is undeniable. Influential people only hold influence over our lives if we choose to bend to their will. Even the tyrant who wields an iron fist in our work or home life are little more than the emperor with his new clothes. In *The Emperor's New Clothes*, it took a child to point out the obvious: the emperor was butt naked. The child in that story is there to remind us that while an influential person can shape the world around them, even they can't escape the blinding truth of reality: they only hold an illusion of power. The real power in our lives rests with us.

Our daily decisions determine the success or failure of the businesses on our high streets. Our actions in the secrecy of the ballot box decide what kind of government we get. And our thoughts and emotions determine what type of society we build.

Movie moguls, dictators, exploitative businesses and corrupt public figures forget a fundamental fact at their peril. We don't have to watch their movies, buy their products, listen to their lies or accept their rule.

Your natural state is to be free. As Martin Luther King said, "The arc of the moral universe is long, but it bends towards justice." As one year ends and a new one begins, we hope you break free of the chains that bind you to a life far from your dreams. And we hope that you remember the power of your dreams. You may only be one person, but you can remake our world. May your dreams become a reality in 2018

THE LEOPARD
Paul D. McDonagh

I pity the leopard for he cannot change
his spots. He must look upon you
with wonder and awe. That you are so free

to keep your spots and the stories they tell
of your life or to change them at will;
at least redefine them in your own eyes

not as blemishes to be hidden or forgotten,
but as moments of truth full of meaning
lost until you become willing to learn.

Jack London

"A bone to the dog is not charity. Charity is the bone shared with the dog, when you are just as hungry as the dog."

9

Craighead Christmas Message 2018

Whether or not you believe in the religious significance of Christmas is not the point. Many human cultures, from the Druids to the Romans, have had a shared celebration at this time of the year. Our current shared celebration happens to be called Christmas. Of course, if the Druids were still running the show, it would no doubt be called something utterly unpronounceable in one of the Celtic languages. Given this, it's clear there is a deep need within us to mark the winter solstice.

Perhaps a celebration at the time of the winter solstice isn't about the presents we receive. Perhaps it keeps our minds from thinking about the cold nights that lie ahead and allows us to spend time with friends and family we may not see the rest of the year. Yes, Christmas is over-commercialised, but it is also true that we would pay any price to have one more Christmas with the person who is no longer with us.

Christmas may not always be a happy time for us. We may suffer some of the bitterest losses imaginable at this time of the year. But we also recognise when we offer a kind word to friends and strangers and hope for better things for others that we are all connected, we are all branches in the tree of humanity.

Just as a tree may lose its leaves and seem lifeless during winter, it is true to say that even in the deepest winter of the soul, we know instinctively that from the darkness comes light. With darkness all around us, it's worth remembering that it's our inner light, our hope for happier times to come that we celebrate most at this time of the year. And it is this that transforms us from the caterpillar on the leaf we feel we have become into the butterfly we are capable of being.

We leave you this year with a poem about a tree. Like the trees you see at the edge of the car parks or outside some of the flats in Craigheads that renew themselves each year in difficult conditions, we hope you come to realise that you can renew yourself in the New Year, even if you feel like a tree stuck in stony ground.

THE TREE
Paul D. McDonagh

Perhaps the tree you saw
on your walk home from work
wasn't just a tree but a metaphor
for the divine.

Perhaps God doesn't have a beard
like we sometimes imagine
or speak to us from burning bushes.

Perhaps God is the tree
that provides shade for the lamb,
a place to nest for birds with hungry chicks
and a home for squirrels
sleeping through winter.

Like a tree, perhaps God's shape
and form feeds the hungry
insects and vision-starved poet,
and gives the musician an instrument
whose sound expresses their passion.

Perhaps God is a tree
and each star is like a branch
sticking out from the trunk
and each planet merely a leaf
and we the caterpillar
munching on that leaf
waiting to turn into a butterfly.

Abraham Lincoln

"The probability that we may fail in the struggle ought not to deter us from the support of a cause we believe to be just."

Craighead Christmas Message 2019

For some, this Christmas is filled with love and happiness that comes from spending time with those they love most. For other people, this Christmas is filled with worry over unpaid bills, the grief from losing a close friend or relative or the loneliness that comes from having friends and family who live too far away to visit.

Whatever choices and decisions you've made over the last year and whoever you have lost along the way, it can seem that people are swept up in festive cheer while you're in a darkness from which there is no escape. Yet the darkness you see around you is like the shadow cast by the light within you. Your light still burns as brightly as a sun, and it will guide your way. Your pain and sorrow may stick to you like a shadow, but it also mirrors the light of the love you give to all those around you. You know that in your pain and suffering, you can choose to connect with those around you, choose to help them and in so doing, remind yourself that you are not alone.

We all suffer losses throughout life. We lose the people we love and the people we love then lose us eventually, too. It is the price we pay for choosing to love. And while we cannot comfort those we leave behind, we can comfort those around us who carry the burden of grief, the worry of unpaid bills and the pain of regret that comes from things unsaid or undone.

THE DUCK
Paul D. McDonagh

Inspired by events in the life of Jimmy McHaffie

Such a strange creature is the duck.
It's almost like God got the angels one day
to make him something in his workshop
for a laugh just to see what they'd do.

As they scratched their halos and looked about,
they must have found webbed feet and a pair of wings
lying on a worktop or in some obscure drawer.

They took what they found and stuck them on something
with two eyes and a bill and then chucked on some feathers
that had been lying around since the day before
he made the peacock.

When God saw what the angels had made,
he burst into laughter for a god needs to have a sense
of humour to understand and love all of creation.

God looked it over and chuckled to himself,
for he was pleased to find some things were still a surprise.
God smoothed down the duck's feathers
and carried it to Earth and set it upon the water
next to the Tree of Knowledge in the Garden of Eden.

As God turned to take his leave, he winked at the duck
and heard it quack for the very first time and smiled,
for although he sensed what was crawling in the grass,
he knew everything was going to be all right in the end
because even the duck had found its place in paradise.

Seneca

"We never reflect how pleasant it is to ask for nothing."

11

Craighead Christmas Message 2020

When we started the year, we couldn't have predicted we would spend weeks and months alone unable to visit our friends and family, and then spend time queuing outside our local supermarket just to buy the essentials. You could even say that the coronavirus is like the kind of virus that brought down the alien invaders in H.G. Wells' *The War of the Worlds*. Yes, with having to wear masks inside shops and public buildings and many of our everyday activities limited, this year has felt somewhat apocalyptic, like something from the pages of H.G. Wells' science fiction book or even one of those dystopian novels written by Aldous Huxley and George Orwell. But despite all the drastic changes to our lives, we have endured. You have endured. And the speed with which scientists have developed a vaccine in the last nine months proves the ingenuity of humanity. This can comfort us as we wait for the vaccine programme to be rolled out across the country and protect our most vulnerable friends and family members.

Of course, beyond the scientific breakthroughs and advancements in medical knowledge in tackling the coronavirus, our own individual achievements are no less significant. For some of us, the time away from our regular routine has helped us finish a novel, learn to play a musical instrument or speak a foreign language. For others, it has led to a new exercise regime or to using new technology to chat via Zoom, Skype or Facetime and form new habits to break old ones. Of course, for others, this year hasn't meant spending time learning a new skill or producing something like a painting or a book. Instead, for many others, this year has been a complicated process of learning to recreate themselves.

Those who have been furloughed for months will have had to ask themselves the question: who am I when I am not working? Those who can't travel abroad, go to their social clubs or visit their favourite events and exhibitions as they would like have had to ask themselves who am I when I am not around other people? And for those that have lost a loved one but were unable to attend their funeral, they had to ask themselves how do I grieve for the one I loved when I cannot mourn as I would like? Whether it be the loss of a job, a way of life or a loved one, these major shifts in life can be overwhelming and lead to depression and anxiety and be especially difficult at a time when we can't easily reach out to those closest to us.

For many of us, this year has been an emotional desert. With worries over our livelihoods, relationships, and the losses we have suffered along the way, that desert has turned into a desert of despair. But despite what we have been through, and despite the weeks and months of waiting ahead of us that may seem to slip through the hourglass of time like grains of sand, perhaps there is an oasis of hope in this desert that we can find in our minds, especially if we must spend Christmas alone this year.

ROUTE 66
Paul D. McDonagh

All those farmhands
John Steinbeck wrote about
in Grapes of Wrath
travelled along Route 66,
tried to stay one step
ahead of the Dust Bowl
and the Depression
but failed and died
in the end.

Their lives, their dreams
of the land that once sustained them
became like grains of sand in a desert.

But from the desert comes hope,
for when there's nothing
but shifting sand under your feet
and only the will to keep going,
you become like Moses.

You must wander through the desert
of life with nothing but a vision
to sustain you while all around you
everyone has stopped believing
in you and in themselves.

Yet on the old highway signposts
on Route 66, which still stand like old men
with failing memories of who they used to be,
the truth is still there, though hidden:

You come to know the Promised Land
not because you have had a vision
from God but because you have had
to spend years travelling through the desert.

Pindar

"Every gift which is given, even though it be small, is in reality great, if it is given with affection."

12

Craighead Christmas Message 2021

Like the two old town boys who go on a crazy ride along with Bill Murray's character in the film *Groundhog Day*, you can be forgiven for thinking that every day since the pandemic started has been the same. You can be forgiven for thinking it has been nothing more than a never-ending series of mask-wearing events, vaccine injections and news stories of new variants that may or may not make all those actions meaningless. And that, in the face of all the restrictions imposed on you, nothing you do matters. But you're mistaken. What you do does matter, especially to your friends and family. Indeed, as Bill Murray's character realised, if you are stuck in your own personal time loop, where everything you do doesn't matter, you have the freedom to make small changes to your life every day. After all, if what you do doesn't matter, then it doesn't matter if you try something new and make a fool of yourself because nothing you do matters, right? Of course, you're not in a time loop. It only feels that way sometimes. So, take heart and remember that, just like water erodes rock over time, you can move even the most difficult of problems in your life if only you put your shoulder to the task.

Perhaps the lockdowns we've experienced over the last year might explain why millions of people just like you have quit their jobs, put down the masks they've been wearing over their souls and are trying to find work attuned to their true selves. Perhaps the gift the pandemic has given us is time away from our daily routines, time and space to step back from our lives to see if the way we have lived up until now has made us happy. Perhaps it has helped us see what we want to do when this long winter of the soul ends.

Of course, if you feel trapped, just like Bill Murray's character, feel like a prisoner in your life, it begs the question: who is the prison guard? You may not like us for saying this one bit, but the person who is trapping you in an unhappy life is You! It's your feelings, your thoughts and your beliefs about life that are making you unhappy, not the universe outside your head. The world can be brutal and unforgiving at times, but physical pain and suffering are nothing compared to the pain you experience from your thoughts, feelings and beliefs.

Echoing much of the sentiments in *Groundhog Day*, Viktor Frankl, in his book *Man's Search for Meaning*, gives a detailed account of the treatment he and his fellow prisoners experienced at the hands of Nazi guards. He recalls in vivid detail how some people couldn't cope with the unjust treatment they received. Seeing no escape from their tormentors, some of his fellow prisoners committed suicide. They grabbed onto the electric fences around the camp and electrocuted themselves or simply refused to eat and so starved to death. Frankl asked himself the question: why are some people able to endure the horrors of the death camps while others cannot? He discovered that the reason wasn't necessarily because they were the strongest, bravest or most intelligent individuals. No, it was those prisoners who had some ultimate meaning in their lives that endured the worst conditions of the concentration camps. As Frankl said, "Everything can be taken from a man but one thing: the last of the human freedoms – to choose one's attitude in any given set of circumstances, to choose one's own way."

Fortunately, we will never have to endure the horrors that Viktor Frankl experienced. But for many of us who bear the ordinary misery the pandemic has brought, we can quickly come to feel like we're living the same day over and over again. Our escape from this feeling is to recognise that, while our lives may seem like prisons without bars, we are free. Despite all the pain and suffering still to come our way, we know we can make small changes that cause many ripples over time. We can put our shoulders to the task of life, and we can stubbornly refuse to give up our ultimate freedom – the freedom to choose our own way, to choose our own meaning in life. And if we can do that, we can break free of the chains that bind us to unhappiness and put down the masks over our hearts so we can be our authentic selves even if we still must wear masks over our faces for months to come.

BE YOURSELF
Paul D. McDonagh

"Be Yourself. The world worships the original." **Ingrid Bergman**

Like a lily in a pond
Like a bird in its nest
Like a dog with a stick
Or a cat with a mouse
Be yourself.

Like a lily floating on water
Like a bird flying in the sky
Like a dog wagging with joy
Or a cat in love with the chase
Be yourself.

"We have two ears and one mouth so that we can listen twice as much as we speak."

13

Craighead Christmas Message 2022

With three British prime ministers in a single year, a cost-of-living crisis across the globe and a war in Europe, all hot on the heels of a pandemic that affected us deeply, it can feel that the world is going to hell. At the very least, it can sometimes feel like we have regressed to the 1930s when dictators threaten to march us towards a world war. Just as a deep economic depression takes root in the lives of millions of ordinary people like us who must choose between heating or eating this winter, the world has grown hungry for war. It feels that the words of W. B. Yeats, "The centre cannot hold," are echoing in the wind. Indeed, the words of Mark Twain ring true more now than at any other time. "History never repeats itself, but it does often rhyme."

Although the past cannot change, we are still free to change our fate because the future is not predetermined. The future is written every day through our actions in the present. As Scrooge from *A Christmas Carol* realised, *"Men's courses will foreshadow certain ends, to which, if persevered in, they must lead. But if the courses be departed from, the ends will change.'* At a time when it seems the centre of our lives cannot hold, that the plans we thought were solid are crumbling before our eyes, it is important more than ever to realise the power we have in shaping our destiny and that of those around us.

We know you can hold the line against the darkness in the world because something in your heart calls out to our better angels. As Abraham Lincoln said when he saw his country divided and a war on the horizon, "We are not enemies, but friends. We must not be enemies. Though passion may have strained, it must not break our bonds of affection but swell the chorus of the better angels of our nature."

If you do not already know because no one told you, we hope you realise that you are one of the better angels Lincoln spoke about. You are an angel in the many ways you look out for your friends and family. Though this winter may be cold and unforgiving, we hope you realise that just like an angel, you bring your light to the darkness. And you can cast out the shadows of worry and anxiety into the night with the light that burns brightly in your heart.

THE ANGEL
Paul D. McDonagh

An angel looked down at Earth
from the highest point in heaven
and thought what he saw was good.

He saw the animals in the forest,
the birds in the sky and the humans
in their cities and yearned to see more.

He lept from the highest point of heaven
with wings spread wide like his heart and flew
to Earth to know more of the mortal creatures

so loved by the other angels observing
the ebb and flow of creation like others might gaze
upon the stars and imagine what is unfolding

in the impossible distances of space separating them.
Yet heaven is a strange place where time works differently
and what mortals call a lifetime flies by

in the blink of an angel's searching eye.
But still, the angel flew onwards
closer to the creatures he would know

and that changed with each breath they took.
Maybe the angel wanted to look upon the face of God.
For you see, God is not as humans perceive him.

God is the ebb and flow of the tides,
the outstretched branches of a tree
that shade the lamb, nourishes the insects

and shelters the creatures that would nest in it.
God does not exist outside of life but through it.
God is everything that has lived and will ever live.

And God dies when life itself dies. The angel flew
onwards towards Earth, gathering speed and heard
life call out to him when he was no longer flying but falling.

As the angel plummeted through the atmosphere,
his wings started to catch fire and his feathers fell
off just like those from Icarus's waxed wings did long ago.

But the angel did not drown in the sea as Icarus did.
Instead, as he hurled to the ground, he found
the trees in the forest reaching out to catch him.

He woke dazed and confused, dangling from a branch
by his halo. Before he could do anything else, the branch
snapped, and the little chicks in the nest above laughed

for they thought the angel a strange bird indeed.
When the angel thumped to the forest floor,
he experienced pain for the very first time.

He wept then not just because his halo was bent
or because his body ached the way a mortal's does.
No, he wept because his wings had burned away.

The angel wept for what he had lost and feared
he would never reach heaven again.
Nothing much remained of the angel's wings

but for a few charred feathers that stank of brimstone.
Still, an angel's tears are not like those of mortals,
for an angel's grief brings forth life, not relief from death.

As his tears hit the ground, flowers began to bloom,
and birds came to chirp and tweet around him.
But the angel's broken-heartedness made him blind.

He did not see the trail of beauty he left in his wake,
did not hear the birds sing and gladden the hearts
of mortals dealing with woes that end in death.

Soon the angel had walked the Earth completely.
On his way, he discarded his bent and discoloured halo,
threw it into a muddy field where it sank without trace.

He replaced his muddied and torn gown, too, with robes
fit for humans in their cities full of noise and bluster.
The angel now looked and behaved like a mortal human.

And the more human he became, the more the angel's powers faded.
The trail of flowers that once sprung up from the ground
with each footstep faded in time from flowers to weeds

then to nothing at all. The birds stopped chirping, too,
because he no longer enchanted them with his tears.
He could no longer even sing to them of his sorrow.

Like a musician with a busted guitar, something fell
silent in him that was deafening to some
of the creatures once drawn to him.

Soon all the angel saw was the beastliness in man:
the casual cruelty, betrayal and lack of compassion.
He held his contempt for humanity close and nursed it.

He was an angel far from heaven who had forgotten
that an angel was more than wings and a halo.
They were the messengers, not of God but of Life.

He was the way Life tries to tell the story
Of itself to itself. Although the angel had forgotten,
his essence still burned like a sun within him

that could never be destroyed. For an angel is Meaning
in its purest form which can never be destroyed only lost
until found.

As the years flowed by, the angel's vision narrowed,
until he found himself retreating from humans completely
his only comfort found in the gentleness of animals

54

that would come and listen to him talk of what he had lost.
But even the animals that came left him for they knew
they could not help an angel see that all of life must be wept over

not just part of it. They knew mortal beings must face
the death of those they love and then face their own death
and the grief they cause those they leave behind.

Then one day, the angel ventured out for the sun in the sky
and the birds in the clouds called to him. He was anxious
for he had not stood with humans in centuries and the world

had become a swarm of bees buzzing with noise and haste
since last he walked. As they buzzed around him, he felt
the need to close his eyes and return to where he had slept

for centuries. Despite his discomfort, he kept his eyes open
and saw things anew despite his pain. He saw a child laugh
as a dog licked their face and an old couple smile

as they weathered the storms of old age and held hands,
and he saw the youths with their strange manners laugh
not at him but at the joy of each other's company.

And the more he looked, the more the angel saw.
He saw, despite their suffering, these mortals faced
life with love and used the pain in the hidden parts

of their souls to remake the world for those they loved.
And then as he looked deeper into their souls, he saw feathers
and then wings, too, which flapped when they dreamed

of better things for others. And then the angel broke down
for he remembered he was an angel, and as he wept,
flowers sprung up from his tears and an incredible agony

overcame him as bone shot out from his back and formed
into wings. The humans near him only saw a mortal man
falling and did not know that the angel had his wings.

As they helped him to his feet, the angel smiled at them,
not just because he had his wings and could return to heaven
but because he knew now what angels are.

As he left the Earth and flew up to heaven, the angel laughed
for he understood why all the angels in heaven loved
to look upon the unfolding mystery of life.

The angel soared onwards through the gates of heaven
into the meeting place of the angels to tell them the truth
that their love is the greatest of the mortal strengths.

That they were all mortal once, too, and had only forgotten
just as he had forgotten he was an angel
and that it is love which transforms mortal creatures into angels.

14

The Future of the Craighead Christmas Message

The future of the Craighead Christmas Message is bright because you have bought this book. As it costs me around £50-£100 each year to print and deliver the message to people living in Craighead Housing Estate, I appreciate that you chose to buy a copy of this book. That decision may seem minor to you, but it helps put this project on a secure footing. If I sell loads of copies of this book, I could expand the project and fund future community projects. In the meantime, encourage others to download the e-book or order a paperback edition from Amazon to spread a little Christmas cheer much further.

Acknowledgements

I want to acknowledge the people of Craighead Housing Estate and all those that have enjoyed reading the messages. Without you, this project would not exist.

As well as being the author of The Craighead Christmas Messages, Paul D. McDonagh is a poet and life story writer. He has worked with dozens of residents in care homes across Scotland to write their life stories.

He is also the author of A State of Independence, Diamond in the Rough, Write Your Autobiography the Easy Way and A Man Called Uncle.

FOR MORE INSPIRATIONAL TITLES
Visit www.astateofindependence.com
A home for the independent spirit

Printed in Great Britain
by Amazon

13963164R00036